HOW TO START A START-UP

How To Start a Business and Profit on a Shoestring Budget

by Perry Belcher

Published By Shoestring Press Publishing

4500 Spanish Oaks Club Blvd.

Austin Texas USA

512-971-5049

To order additional copies of this book please call 1-512-971-5049

ISBN 978-1-937126-03-2

Library of Congress Catalog –PENDING

Belcher, Perry.

How to Start a Start-Up : How To Start a Business and Profit on a Shoestring Budget / by Perry Belcher

p. cm.

Includes bibliographical references and index.

ISBN 978-1-937126-03-2

1. Business

About The Author

Perry Belcher is a serial entrepreneur, author, publisher, copywriter, marketer, SEO expert, importer and business coach from Austin, Texas.

Perry has imported, manufactured, created and sold more than $100,000,000 in merchandise, information and services over his career.

Perry is an author of 11 books and courses on business in just the past few years.

He is also a devoted husband and father to two daughters and two sons, and the worst guitar player in all of Texas.

Today, Perry is semi-retired and spends most of his time these days consulting with and investing in mid-sized businesses where he can add the greatest value.

In addition, Perry has been a keynote speaker at many business and marketing functions.

To hire Perry, please contact Sandy Bradshaw at 512-555-1212

Contact Perry through social media

twitter.com/perrybelcher
perrybelcher.com/facebook
youtube.com/perrybelcher

or read Perry's blog at perrybelcher.com

Contents

So, you're about to start a business. You're not sure what you're going to do yet, but you want advice about how to do it.

In this guide are all the steps you have to take to start a business: the planning steps, the pre-planning steps, and all the groundwork you need to lay before you get started.

Disclaimer

This is my opinion of how I would go about setting up a new business and how I have done it in the past. I am not a lawyer, I am not an accountant, and I am not any kind of a licensed professional, so before you get started in any of these fields, you need to consult your attorney or your accountant to make legal decisions, particularly about things that have to do with your individual state and local government regulations because that can get you in a lot of hot water. I wouldn't want you to take any information from here and take it as legal advice because it is not legal advice. It is just general information and my opinion.

I'm going to describe people who make a lot of money and some who don't make any money. I'm not making any income promises. I'm not going to tell you that if you do things my way, you are going to make a whole bunch of money, or if you do things my way, you are going to go broke. That depends on how you run your business and how much you want to work, and how smartly you do what you do. If I talk about a guy who made $100,000 in some business, that means that's how much *he* made. It doesn't mean that you necessarily are going to, although you may very well make much, much more.

Legal Framework 1

One of the first questions people thinking of starting a business in the US ask is: "Do I need a lawyer?"

My recommendation would be, probably.

Lawyers don't have to be greatly expensive. You can get a good general practicing lawyer on retainer usually for less than $1000. I try to use guys who are single office attorneys, initially, that are running a small business just like you, so they understand the strains of the business.

Explain that you want general advice from them. There might be ways to cut corners in places where you don't necessarily need a lawyer, but it is always good to have one, especially if you are planning to incorporate or if you are going to need to draw up contracts in the business you are in.

Perhaps there is potential in your business for somebody suing you. I know some friends that are in the food business and if I were in the food business, I would definitely want to have a lawyer on retainer pretty much all the time.

I've got a friend who owns restaurants, and he has 60 franchise restaurants. In 60 franchise restaurants, there is going to be a level of food poisoning cases. They have a certain level that they expect to have every year of food poisoning cases. If they go over, they get kind of worried. If it is under that level, they have a big party. In a case like this, you always want an attorney on staff.

Liability

If you are in a business where there is a particular danger involved, one of the things that was told to me one time a long time ago was that poison-makers usually don't have to take out a lot of insurance. The idea is that you know it is poison when you pick it up. Let people know that they are in a dangerous situation, and that takes away a lot of your liability (although anywhere children are involved, you will still usually get in trouble).

In my experience, you get in more trouble if a person is in a situation where they don't think they are at risk, and they have the potential of being harmed somehow. In this situation, there's a false sense of security. If there is a danger about, let people know. That's going to help you a whole lot with your liabilities.

At skate parks, for instance: these kids at skate parks get bumped up and bruised all the time, but they known that when they go in. They have all these great big signs and disclaimers saying: “Hey, you can get hurt here.”

For the most part, the skate park owners are relatively shielded from liability. However, that doesn’t mean they are not going to get sued. A person can sue you for just about anything, and they do.

Picking Your Lawyer

Almost everybody knows somebody in the business. So, take a successful business person who has been a successful business person for a while, and ask their advice. Say: “I am going into business. I am looking for a lawyer. Do you know somebody I could use that is not going to charge me an arm and a leg and that is a decent guy?" I can think of three people off the top of my head right now that I would recommend to somebody.

If you do that, you are probably going to be okay. Remember this: if you get recommended by a big client, they are less likely to screw you over because it makes them look bad to their big client. If you just walk in, if you pick a guy out of the phone book and he decides to put the hose to you, he really doesn't have a whole lot to lose.

You want to tie into another client. Get a friend of your parents or a friend of a friend of a friend who has got a relationship. Go to somebody that you know and get a resource from them or get a reference from them, rather than just picking somebody at random based on how big their Yellow Pages ad is.

Working With A Partner

Another thing to be mindful of when staying out of legal trouble, beyond just having a lawyer on retainer, involves contracts and dealing with partners. This is a big area that there is a lot of conflict in.

People who are starting businesses tend to want to start up with someone else for the help. It's also more fun, and it feels like you are at less risk if you are doing it with somebody else.

I see a lot of businesses that get into legal messes because of partnerships that are handshake deals. A lot of times you are in business with a friend, and a lot of times a really close friend or relative. You think: "I don't need a contract to do this."

Really, I would say you need a contract there far more than you need it anywhere else. You need to sit down and really set the expectations of what each person's role is up front and get it in writing. That will save you a whole lot of trouble on the back end. I think that is one of the biggest areas, as you have a lot more at stake than just the business. You've got your friendship.

The Give Or Take Test

You need to work out the criteria on the front end for what each person will bring to the partnership. Everybody needs to have an equal upside and an equal downside. Eventually, if you don't have that, one of the parties is going to end up in a slight. If one person is doing a whole lot more work than the other, then that person is going to feel taken advantage of. If one person puts up all of the investment and the other person puts up nothing, that person is going to feel taken advantage of.

You need to really lay it all out and say: "Is this fair?" One of the easiest tests for that is the give or take test.

If you ever have a partner you want to dissolve and get out of business with, basically you write down a figure on a piece of paper, and you say: "I will either buy you out for this amount, or I will take this amount to get out."

Nothing could be any fairer in the world than that.

For your business, you could divide up the responsibilities that cost the investment, lay it out on the table and say: "Look, you pick which half you want, and I will do the other half."

That way you are really getting fairness. You are letting the other side choose. For the most part, that makes for a much better transaction on your side. It makes you write things out in a very balanced way because they may say: “No, why don’t you take this side?”

It’s also good with buy/sell agreements. Your partner, for instance, if you ever decide to buy them out, you say: “Hey, I will give you $50,000 to buy you out.” The first thing that pops into their mind is: “I bet it is worth a whole lot more than that.”

“Well, if it is, then just buy me.”

You can’t beat the fairness of that. You are giving them the option.

Clear Responsibilities

Going into the agreement with it mapped out exactly what you are going to do and exactly what they are going to do is great. Plans change though, as you move through. A business is a living organism. Things change.

What destroys more partnerships and more agreements is when things are changing and not being addressed on a real regular basis. Just be clear with your partner and say: “If you ever feel in the slightest way like there is any part of this business that is unfair to you or me or whatever, please voice it to me.” And be willing to do the same thing yourself.

What often happens is passive/aggressive behavior. People allow things to continue for a long period of time, and then they explode or turn off completely.

I was in a business one time. My partner had a particular behavior, and over a period of time it really just irked me to the point that I just hated the business. One day I just went in and said: “You know, I am leaving. Buy me out." I sold out for almost nothing, and I left. The business probably got stunted in its growth and would have been a better business, but I was at a point where I didn't care any more. This wasn't over a major slight, it was over a relatively minor thing, but things like that fester.

If we had been in communication or had a better structure, that could have been avoided. Think about it like a marriage. If you go into business with somebody, you are probably going to spend more time with that person than you are going to spend with your wife or your husband.

If your wife did something you didn't like, or your husband did something that you didn't like, you would say: "That really makes me feel bad when you do that. I wish you wouldn't do that anymore. I don't think this is fair," and let them know up front so they could have the ability to adjust the behavior. That seems to take care of 90 percent of the problems.

Trademark and Copyright Law

In a lot of cases, you are going to need copyrights and trademarks in your business. Again, this gets into an area where it is very legal. I am going to give you a very general, broad overview because there is no way I can advise you in your particular situation.

The biggest thing I will tell you is that there is a big confusion between copyrights and trademarks. People don't understand what the two are.

Trademarks

A trademark is a mark for a name or a sales message that you have. A slogan, so to speak, can be trademarked. A brand name can be trademarked. It could, quite literally, be the name of your business.

An image can be trademarked, like the Nike swoosh. If you ever want to get sued real quickly, put that on anything, even something that looks like it. Don't make a checkmark too loosely on anything, or you will get sued by Nike.

That is a trademark and trademarks have a considerably different way of being enforced. You have to file a trademark application. It has to be approved, but during that time you are somewhat protected.

There is also an assumed trademark in different states. Different states have state trademark laws. For the most part—and this is not true in all states—but in a lot of states, if you have a particular name for your business, the secretary of state protects that name so no other business in the state can have the same name of yours.

The principle of trademark law is the idea of "confusingly similar". For instance, if I wanted to start a new soft drink company and call it Coca-Kola, that wouldn't work out. You can't do that. People think: "I'm going to spell it with a K instead of a C." It doesn't matter: they are confusingly similar. If your intent is to confuse the consumer, which obviously it would be, then you are probably going to get into trouble.

The good news is that if you are a trademark holder, you can pretty loosely enforce it around things like that to the point that if somebody gets a name kind of close to yours, you can attack them if you want to. Courts tend to find in favor of trademark holders, so trademark holders have a lot of juice. Trademarks typically will help keep competitors from using your name and things like that. They don't give monetary damages in trademark cases as often as they do in other cases like patent cases and things like that.

The assumption is overall if you are starting a business, try to do something that had never been heard of before. Be creative, be unique.

The U.S. Patent and Trademark office (www.USPTO.gov) has a searchable database of trademarks. You can search them by spelling, but only by spelling. You ought to search any way somebody could possibly spell your name and see if there was someone who could have a name that is confusingly similar. Put in all the bad spellings.

I did a project not too long ago called Isogel, which was an isopropyl alcohol gel. There is a company in Denmark with a similar product who had filed a U.S. trademark called Iceogel.

We had 300,000 bottles of our product on the market. We had done a trademark search to make sure nobody was named Isogel. We filed a trademark application for Isogel.

They found us by our trademark application. They saw it in the Trademark Gazette that we had applied for that trademark, and they opposed the trademark and made us have a recall on our product. It cost us a lot of money.

You can definitely land in hot water. There are companies you can pay. If you just go to Google and search "trademark search," there are companies you can pay to do trademark searches that really know what they are doing. They take all the different variables and all of that.

Make sure to research that, because that can be pretty frustrating getting a name out there and then having to go back and change it. If you build your brand up for a year or two and get it up locally and then find out that you can't expand nationally because you don't have the right to use the name, that really bites.

Copyright

Copyright is completely different.

Copyrights protect intellectual property like writings, photos, videos, audio recordings, and things like that. You can't really copyright your name. Again, I am not a lawyer. I don't *think* you can copyright your name.

A copyright of a slogan is kind of tricky because slogans are multi-word, but there are certain limitations. There are a certain amount of words or words used in combination that have to be used to

make a printed copyright. I don't know exactly what that is.
Again, in general, you trademark names and slogans and logos, and you copyright images, videos, audio recordings, and written content or text. You could copyright a brochure, but you trademark the logo on the front of the brochure if you want to be fully protected.

Copyright laws, unlike trademark laws, are easy to enforce. They are fast, and they come with big, fat, nasty penalties. People get stung hard when they violate copyright laws.

Usually the smaller guys have more power to enforce their copyright than they do their trademark.

What sucks about having a trademark and having to enforce it is that if somebody violates your trademark, you can go to a lawyer, and the lawyer says: "Yeah, they violated your trademark. I will go sue them for you for $20,000."

That kind of sucks. You thought you had everything with this trademark, and you could just send them a letter and they would stop. But not necessarily. Sometimes you've got to spend a little money to enforce your trademarks. It is a little less expensive to enforce a copyright.
It is something you should do sooner rather than later. Definitely look into it. If you are not going to trademark right away – it costs three or four hundred dollars to file a trademark application online – you are probably going to have to eventually get a lawyer to help you follow through with it.

A lot of people I know file trademark applications on their own online with the U.S. Patent and Trademark Office. It is a pretty short application. You will usually get back a letter later. They deny most trademark applications on the first attempt just kind of blanket.

You are going to have to provide more proof that you should own it, that somebody else doesn't have anything like it. You are probably going to have to get a lawyer somewhere throughout the trademark process, but you can get the ball rolling on your own if you want.

Composing A Business Plan Think Small 2

The biggest mistake people make with business plans is trying to make them a book. They really try to make a business plan enormous.

I was at a seminar in Seattle, Washington, a few years ago, and I met this guy named Guy Kawasaki that a lot of people know. He is a really nice guy. He was the CFO of Apple computer, and the CFO of Microsoft.

He is a short, Japanese guy, and he said: "I'm the only guy in the audience who has had the privilege of working for both Bill Gates and Steve Jobs. I used to be six foot, four." They beat him down that much!

He is a really brilliant guy, as you would imagine he would be, having both those jobs. He talked a lot about business plans and one of the things that he said was that a business plan should always fit on a sheet of paper, one sheet of paper.

Most people go, “Huh? That is crazy.” But I have seen these things that are executive summaries and not longer than one sheet of paper. If you have to use the back of the sheet of paper, that is the absolute most you should do.

He showed one of the best business plans that he had ever seen. It was on the back of a business card. They basically drew their whole business plan on the back of a business card, and that is how they pitched to VC companies. That is how they got VC funding for $10 million in two weeks.

The second part of a business plan is to have it down to an elevator pitch. In the time it takes to ride from the first floor to the tenth floor in a building, you should be able to tell somebody all about your business.

The Company Profile

The first thing that most business plans start with is creating the company profile. The company profile is a fancy word for: "What do you do?" What do you do? And what makes it unique?

The thing that most people miss in business planning, this portion anyway, is they say, "I am going to be a doggie bakery," or "I am going to be a daycare center," or "I am going to be a carwash." But the world is full of car washes. What is going to make yours particularly special? What is going to make yours different? What is going to make yours unique?

That is a place for you to think, "We want to be a carwash, but here is our hook." In today's business world, if you don't have a particular twist to whatever it is that you are doing, you stand a real risk of not doing very well. The companies that are excelling out there right now are carving out new pieces, meeting new needs, totally new segments of the market.

I think there is a really good opportunity for tons of businesses to adapt to the new economy, to adapt to new personalities of brand-new buyers, and come up with a new way to deliver the same service.

Maybe you have a revolutionary breakthrough. But they are rare. Don't feel depressed if you don't have giant, change-the-world, nobody's-ever-done-this business. In fact, nobody's-ever-done-this statements usually scare the crap out of venture capital guys.

“I’ve got a great idea! Nobody’s ever done it!”

Well, there is usually a reason nobody’s ever done it. Usually it’s that nobody’s ever done it *that you’ve heard of*. Most things have been tried or attempted by somebody, and a lot of it just fell on absolute disaster.

It is more about getting in there and figuring out how you are going to distinguish yourself from your competitors, or find a niche that you are going to market that people haven’t marketed that service in before.

Product And Service Analysis

This is where you really get into the details of what makes you special: the unique selling proposition, or USP.

Every business plan should have this. For the doggie bakery example:

> "Yes, we are a doggie bakery, but the second part is what makes us different is we have all the ingredients there, and the pet owners come in and actually make the doggie biscuits for the dogs.
>
> It's an experience, and they get to bring their dogs with them, and the dogs get to hang out and have a good time, and the pet owners get to hang out and have a good time. We have a singles section where they all mix and everybody falls in love!"

We just invented a brand-new business! Doggie biscuit matchmaking.

That is the kind of thing: what is going to be cool about my product, and what is going to be different about it?

Marketing Plan

The first thing you need to do is do a market analysis. That is where a huge percentage of business plans fail because they don't know.

If somebody ever asked you – a business person, a potential partner, a vendor, or a venture capitalist – who will want to buy this? Who is your market? The idiot answer is: "Everybody!"

If that is true (and 99 percent of the time it is not) probably what is going to happen if everybody wants something is that it will become a commodity.

Everybody wants potatoes. There is not a whole lot of money in the potato business unless you are selling hundreds and hundreds of truckloads of potatoes every day. Everybody wants it, and everybody needs it: it is a commodity. Typically it is a volume business, and there are very small margins.

Faberge eggs, on the other hand, there is a particular market of collectors: probably women, probably wealthy, willing to pay whatever. You have to deliver the proper message to the proper market.

Analyzing *who* you are marketing to is probably the most important thing.

The Triad Marketing System

I did a product not long ago with my friend, Ryan Deiss, called The Triad Marketing System. We spent four hours answering that question. It is a pretty big question, but it is something worth learning.

There are really only three ways to build a business.

One is to attract more customers. The second is to get those customers to buy more stuff from you. The third way is to increase the ticket of the purchase every time they buy.

When designing their marketing program, most people only take into account how they are going to get customers. They don’t address the other two.

To a venture capitalist, that is a telltale sign that you don’t know what you are doing. They realize the bulk of the money in a business comes out of a customer you already have.

How are you going to extract more money, or a longer lifetime value, or a LTV, of the customer? Once you have the customer, what are you going to do with him?

Everyone concentrates on how many more customers. But smart money wants to know, when you get more customers, what are you going to do with them? You need to figure out a way to stay out in front of the current customers and create either new services or different variations of to keep them coming back.

Before you compose your business plan you should study marketing online. There are a lot of good books out there.

A friend of mine, Dan Kennedy, has a book for $10 or $15 called The Ultimate Marketing Plan that is pretty good. I would say it is better than pretty good. You might check that out. There are also Seth Godin books. Seth is a good marketer. He is pretty good at market planning, especially in a new economy.

Financial Analysis

I wouldn't have a financial analysis done by anyone other than myself if I were starting a business.

I keep talking about venture capital because a lot of people who are putting together business plans are going to somebody saying: "I need money. I want money. This is why I am putting together a business plan."

Unfortunately, most people don't plan their businesses for the purpose of actually planning their business. They plan to get funded, and then they throw the business plan in a drawer somewhere. They forget about it.

However, your venture capital company, your

funder, won't forget about it. They are going to hold you to certain milestones and things.

One of the greatest lines from Guy Kawasaki when I took his course in a seminar on venture capital money and business planning was about VC companies who want to know your one-year, three-year, five-year financial projections. How much are you going to sell? How much profit are you going to make and all of that?

He finally told everybody from the stage: "You know what? Everybody says that these venture capitalists are stupid. They are asking you all of these questions that you couldn't possibly be accurate with in your estimates."

He said: "This is bullshit. We know that five-year financial projections are bullshit, but we want to know the magnitude of your bullshit."

They want to know how much you believe you can do, how far out there you feel you can reach. That is really the whole purpose of financial projections.

They figure you are going to do something less than your projections. If you are only projecting to do a million dollars a year, and you want to borrow $300,000 to $400,000, it doesn't work.

They have a certain amount of ROI they need to make to make their whole thing work. If you are projecting to do $100 million a year, and there is some ring of truth to that, that it might be possible you could do it, then if you miss your mark completely, you might do $20- to $30 million, and it might be worth their investment.

Venture capitalists and bankers are completely different. Nobody goes to banks to borrow money for the most part because the banks don't loan money to small businesses anymore. For the most part, when you are going to borrow money, you are going to borrow it from a venture capitalist or from a private investor or whatever.

Everybody makes the mistake of thinking they need to be very conservative in their estimates. I would strongly advise you not to be conservative in your estimates.

Reach out there for all you think you can do, and state that. Don't make up stuff you don't believe you could do, but reach out there for all you think you can do, do that, and then that venture capitalist is going to stand over you with a stick to make sure you do it. I promise you, they will be up your butt. That is what they do.

They also are going to provide a lot of help to you, if you get the right ones. They can help you to achieve the goals that you have set for them, even if you don't believe you can do them.

It is a way of putting yourself in a position to actually help you succeed, even though it might be a little painful for a while.

Employees

The way you should manage your small business changes as you acquire more employees.

They say in business that you either want three employees, or you want one hundred. Everything in between kind of sucks.

When you start off, you'll start off with a nucleus of people around you. Everybody is going to know everything that is going on in the company. What really changes as you grow is communication, because if you get 20, 30, or 40 people working for you in a business, it is very difficult for all the people to know and to understand what is going on all the time.

I believe that most people in a building should know what is going on. I think it is good, even the employees that don't have an impact directly on what is going on. I think it makes them feel more comfortable, and it makes them feel involved.

If you read exit surveys when people leave companies, the biggest reason they leave is not because their boss was a jerk. It is not because they didn't get paid enough money. It is because they didn't feel involved. They didn't feel their contribution, their input was important to the business. That is the number one reason people leave.

Meet with your people on a regular business. Don't go into a meeting frenzy, try to keep them as informal as you can. I am a real big believer in social gatherings, pizza parties and things like that.

However, there is going to come a time when you just don't want to inform every employee about every aspect of your business.

You are giving up security, for one thing. If a low-level employee goes to work for your competitor, then everything you have taught them or they know about your business is exposed, and they are not going to adhere to any non-compete contracts or gag orders or any of that. They are going to talk, and it will be too late. By the time you get mad at them, all you can do is be mad at them. The damage has been done.

Entrepreneurs vs. Managers

I finally learned the lesson later in life that my goal

is to get a business to a point of being really nicely profitable with seven or eight people and ready to go to the next level, and then I hire in a really good manager, and let them take the company from there.

If you are an entrepreneur and a manager, I would like to meet you because I don't think I have ever met one. Entrepreneurs usually totally suck as managers. Managers usually totally suck as entrepreneurs. The entrepreneur builds the sculpture. The manager can sand it and polish and refine it over time, but he couldn't take that chunk of rock and make a face out of it to save his life. An entrepreneur would get bored senseless by polishing that piece of rock for the next 20 years.

There is a purpose for both sides of business.

Management is extremely important.
Entrepreneurs tend to lack respect for management

people and management people tend to lack respect for entrepreneurs. But basically, without one another, it is very difficult to get by.

If you decide you are going to work with a partner, management partners are usually really easy to find.

If you are the entrepreneurial partner, you are the rock star in the band. There are far fewer of you than there are managers. Typically speaking, managers are happy to find an entrepreneur, and a smart entrepreneur is glad to find a really good manager.

The entrepreneur's candle will burn out very quickly without a good manager to work with. If you look at Steve Jobs, he had Wozniak. Jobs was the entrepreneur, the sales guy, and Woz was the guy that got it all done. Bill Gates had Paul Allen. If you look at most of these mega, mega, mega superstars of business, there was always somebody right there next to them that was making sure everything go done.

A good manager realizes that if they were to lose their vision person, they are screwed. A good entrepreneur will see that if they lost their management, they would be too.

Venture Capital 3

Approaching a Venture Capitalist

Depending on what kind of VC money you are looking for, most VC companies are industry-specific. There are literally just dozens and dozens and dozens of venture capital companies across America. Getting an appointment to see them sometimes is kind of hard.

Write a proposal letter that is one or two paragraphs long, saying: "Hi, I would like to come see you. I have a very unique opportunity. It is not like anything I think you have seen before. It is in this space, and this is our unique selling proposition."

Don't be weird with the VC guys. One thing VC guys never do really is steal ideas. More VC deals get screwed by a guy going, "I want to come show you my idea; I want to get some money."

The VC guy says, “Okay, I will listen to you.”

Then the guy gets paranoid and says: “I will have to bring a contract for you to sign for non-disclosure, non-this and that.”

At this point, the VC guy is like: “Get out of here. I don’t have time to mess with you. You are an idiot. Get out.”

You blew your opportunity protecting an idea that is probably not as good as you think it is. Most of the time the VCs have seen something better than your idea yesterday.

What the most important part is if the VC likes you. The VC can probably be your very best consultant at refining your idea and making it better, saying:

> "Hey, you know what? We've seen a couple of these come through like this. We've even funded one, and here is what happened, and here is why it happened.
>
> If you guys can take your idea and avoid this pitfall the last people made, we think you might have a viable thing, if you're willing to be flexible and make those changes."

If you are willing to listen to advice and just be a real person, they could really help you a lot. I have seen VCs that will see a pitch by somebody, and the pitch doesn't work, but they will call somebody back a month later and say:

> "You know what? We really liked you, and we've got another deal going on right now, and I've got a great entrepreneur, but I don't have a manger. You might be the perfect

> manager for this project. Can you come in and talk to these guys?"

or

> "I've got a group of managers that have this great technology, but they have no vision of how to bring it to market. They need a leader. Would you be interested in coming in and meeting with them?"

A lot of times VCs will put these deals together.

Milestones and Dilution

There is a good and a bad side to venture capitalists. They call them "vulture capitalists" for a reason. Sometimes they are, but for the most part, good venture capital companies have been around a while and are progressive in this economy.

They are not vultures; they just have to protect their investment. They are not going to let you have $10- or $15 million of their money and then go back to their office and wait for you to call them every now and then and say hi.

It doesn't work that way. I am sorry to bust your bubble, but they are going to be there to protect their investment. They are going to set certain milestones for you that you are going to agree to on the front end.

They are going to be high. They are going to be high expectations. They will say: "At the end of three months, you've got to do this, and at six months, you've got to do this. At a year, you've got to do this."

Although it's easy to say you will at the front end, venture capitalists will guarantee it by something called "dilutions."

Say you've got a 50-50 deal. The venture capital company said, "We liked your thing. We will buy half of it for a million dollars." So you own half, and they own half. They put up a million dollars and you are doing your business.

There are going to be milestones in that contract. This is where those projections come in.

> "How much in sales do you think we are going to have in a year?"
>
> "I think we are going to have $3 million in sales."
>
> "Okay. If you miss your milestones and we don't have $3 million in sales, we are going

to dilute you by 20 percent, and you are going to own 30 percent."

If you miss very many milestones, you don't own the company anymore. That is the way that works, but that is your fault. It is your fault for agreeing in the front end, or as we say in the South: "letting your mouth overload your ass."

A lot of people do that especially on the front end because they are just seeing that big check. They want that investment check. Those guys know that. They don't want you to fail.

Venture capitalists, for the most part, are semi-retired people who have been very successful in the past at some business. The last thing they want to do is inherit your crappy little company to come in and run. They do not want that.

If you think their goal is to come in and steal your company, you are wrong. Their goal is for you to perform at what you said you could perform at. Make them a lot of money, make you a lot of money, and everyone will be happy.

It is just not always the way it works out. If you bring somebody out of a lower income situation without managing a lot of money and say: "Here is $10 million dollars; go run this company," a lot of people screw that up.

Financial Management

If you go to venture capitalists without a financial person in place that is experienced, good, and that they can trust, if you get any of your money you are going to leave with one of theirs.

Don't think you are going to get venture capital money and handle it yourself. You are going to have to have somebody who has what they refer to in the industry as 'fiduciary responsibility'.

Someone who is not just impartial but who actually, if they do something wrong, could be in serious legal trouble. They are going to want you to have a licensed CPA, somebody who has a lot to lose if they fudge numbers.

If you don't have one, it is like the court: "If you can't afford an attorney, we are going to assign one to you." If they decide to give you their money, they will not do it under any circumstances unless they are able to place a financial person and the person they place in is probably not going to be as palatable for you as somebody you could bring in yourself.

I would really recommend that if you are putting together a team you need three things: who is going to manage it? Who is going to have the vision? Who is going to count the money?

If you've got those three things going to VC funding, you are miles ahead of most companies.

A Proven Theory

If you are planning on raising money, and if you don't have to raise money from a venture capital company, don't. To go in with a sheet of paper and an idea to raise money from a venture capital company is extremely difficult.

You need to have at least proven your theory. You don't want to walk in the door of a venture capital company and say: "Hi, I've got this idea. In theory, it is going to make $10 million dollars a year."

What they want to see is “I’ve invested $10,000, and I am making $10,000 a month. I think if I invested a million dollars, I would make a million dollars a month based on this experiment that I have performed.”

They want to see that you have already put a little skin into the game and that there is a little bit of a track record there. You’ve proven your theory.

If you walk in with a proven theory, a unique selling proposition, a team and a marketing plan that takes in all three of the triad of how I will get customers, how I will get them to buy more often, and how I am going to get more money per ticket, you are going to get funded. You really are.

Market Size

They are really concerned with market size, too. They want to know how big the general market that you are in is because you could be the king of buggy whips, but there are only so many buggy whips sold nowadays.

If you go in and say: "I am the number one guy in my market. I make $10,000 a month. I have a 70 percent market share, and I want some money," they don't care. They don't want that. They want you to be in a giant market with a sliver of it and a proven way to take more of that market share because they know that at best, you are probably going to have a small piece.
We hear about them. Dell has a giant share in the PC market, and Google has the giant share of the search market, but there are a handful of

companies that have an 800-pound gorilla positioned in their market.

There is a company that we were looking at yesterday called Quinturo which is one of the most expensive laptops you can buy right now: about $2000 when laptops are about $500 or $600. They make a laptop particularly for the gaming market. That is all they do: they make the very best gaming laptop in the world. They knew their market, and they had a unique proposition because it is funky-looking and it is cool. It has a jam-up sound system and killer graphics, and they knew who they were selling to, and they were able to get premium pricing and premium margins.

Being in a really big market but with a highly focused niche isn't a bad thing, especially if there is growth in that niche like in the gaming market. God knows, there is growth there.

Avoiding Failure 4

I was going through a magazine, Business Week, the other day. There was a stat in there that said was that 64% of small businesses are no longer in business after ten years. Not too long ago I read that 95% of Internet Web businesses fail within the first three years. Why are so many small businesses failing?

A lot of it is poor planning and market selection. Market selection is vitally important. I used to be in the retail business. If you look at chain stores, one of their biggest expenditures to building a store is demographics: figuring out where they're going to place that store. They look for where there are a lot of rooftops and conscientious homeowners.

I've been in the direct mail business for years. The most important thing to selling a product by mail order is making sure that you get the message out to the right people.

Most business fail because they don't do the proper amount of research in the frontend: knowing what people want versus guesswork.

We call it the Field of Dreams Business Model: *If I build a restaurant in the middle of nowhere, people will come.*

Competition and Contrast

Right now I have a young lady who works here that has worked for a company that does this continuity model massage business. It's a monthly membership to a massage place and you get a massage or two a month.

One of these businesses is extremely successful. It does a couple of hundred thousand dollars a month. A guy goes down the street, builds another one, hires her away to run it; and, right now he's sitting there with his thumb up his butt and no clients. The reason that he's sitting there with no clients is that the area that he put his shop in is not an affluent area. He has poor visibility, he's not offering the services that the people really want at the prices that they're willing to pay, and he pays no attention to the competition and what he's really up against.

I have a motto: "If you don't have the very best offer in your market place, you're just providing contrast. You are making the other guy look good."

If you have five guys sitting in a row selling rotten apples and one guy is selling beautiful shiny ones, the guy selling the beautiful shiny apples will sell more because the rotten apple guys are there. If you were the only guy there selling semi-rotten apples, you'd probably do okay.

However, if you're sitting next to a guy selling shiny, pretty apples, all things being the same, not even some of the people will say, "I think some of them are going to want shiny apples, some will want rotten." All of them are going to want shiny apples. You're just literally providing contrast for the other guy.

The more competition that's out there that sucks, the better off I'm going to do. That's if I'm on that side of the coin – if I'm the guy with the shiny apples. If I'm the other guy and I just can't get my apples to shine, I'm going to go somewhere where there's just no one else selling apples but me.
Or, maybe just start selling oranges. I'm going to sit there amongst all of the other guys and sell

oranges. At least that way you stand out. You're doing something different and can't be as equally compared.

Finding Your Demographic

I have a buddy who is a dentist. He did a pretty decent amount of research on his particular clients and where he was getting most of his revenue from. Then he actually started following Starbucks. He would set up one of his locations anywhere near where there was a Starbucks.

Piggy-backing demographics are brilliant. We do it in the mail order business all the time. It's not a coincidence that if you get a Cabela's or Orvis catalogs – catalogs which sell outdoor wear for men – then it's not a coincidence that you're going to get other offers in the mail that are male

outdoorsy driven things, because we're going to buy that list.
If I'm in the retail business and I want upwardly mobile professionals that are busy, then I'm going to go plant myself near a Starbucks. If I'm trying to sell something to middle-income families that are trying to get by financially, then I might want to be in a center next to a Wal-Mart.

These companies literally spend hundreds and hundreds of thousands of dollars on just doing demographic work on a location.

One of the funniest to watch are two that I'm sure a lot of people are familiar with: Lowe's and Home Depot. The next time you're at a Home Depot, see if you can't stand in the parking lot and see a Lowe's; most of the time you can. Or, vice versa, or they're on the way. There will be signs sticking up: "The Future Home of Lowe's!" This is because out of all the places to go, this was the optimum 15,000 feet of dirt. Again, they've studied it out and know the best place to build. A friend of mine likens it to walking through a landmine field behind the guy who has been there before. Do you want to just go in yourself and take your chances? Or, do you want to go in behind the guy that's maneuvered around and knows where he's going?

You might still get blown up anyway but that's business and it happens. However, you want to reduce your odds of getting blown up at every possible turn.

However, you don't want to say: "I have a rag doll store and I sell kid's dolls and toys. I'm going to be next to Starbucks because they have great demographics." They have demographics for their market. It's for their market and not necessarily for yours. As long as their market matches up with yours, then that's a good way of doing it.

I used to be in the sign shop business. I used to put sign shops up in the same centers where there was an Office Depot, Office Max, or Staples. This was because I knew that there was a constant flow of small business people coming into there and, for the most part, they use signage. Our customers were business owners so that was a great mix for me.

When you get to piggy-back over everything, you get the leverage out of everyone else's big dollar research.

Business Must-Haves

You're going to need some things that I don't

particularly like doing. However, we all need them.

It's like I said before, you're probably going to need an attorney and some form of business insurance. Even if you don't think you have any liability, you'll need insurance. Almost every business has some sort of liability. You can get some sort of a liability umbrella policy from a local insurance agent and they're typically not too expensive.

A great way to save money on liability insurance is to contact your trade association. In a lot of industries, the trade associations offer liability insurance at a greatly discounted price. It's sometimes as high as 70 to 80% less than buying from a local insurance agent.
If you don't have a financial person on staff right away, you're going to need a bookkeeping service

or some sort of accounting service, to keep up with your books, payroll, payroll taxes, et cetera.

Taxes are incredibly important. If you get behind on your taxes, you're going to have problems, there's just no doubt about that. You want to start off upfront. I would suggest for most people, particularly for payroll taxes, to use employee leasing companies. I'm a big fan of employee leasing companies. Basically, what they do is hire your employees. So, your employees actually work for the employee leasing company. The leasing company that I use charges $50 a month per employee.

For that $50, the employee works for them, they handle all of the taxes and withholding and they send me one bill a month. Then I write them a check. If they're late on the filings for your taxes, then being late with the taxes is their problem. This would free you of the normal $500 to $700 penalty if you were late. The EEOC violations, labor stuff that you have to keep up with, that's all on them. It's a great service for the money.

Make sure that when you start off, you keep your books and records really well. The day you start your business, write your first check and put the first deposit in the bank, say: "You know what? Someday I'm going to sell this business. What is this going to look like to the new buyer?"

Don't ever do anything with your books and records that you wouldn't want a new buyer to see. If you do, you'll find that you'll do a lot worse when it comes time to sell that business, get venture capital for it or bring in a venture partner. It won't make your business unsellable; it'll just make it worth a whole lot less.

It gives them more leverage when they come in because they would have to wade through all of the paperwork. It gives them a reason to discount you.

Withstanding The Dips

If you can, try not to rape your business: don't take out too much money.

With a lot of guys, every time they get $10,000 in the bank, they'll take $9,000 out and try to let the business run on a skeleton all the time. You really don't want to do that. Try to suffer through it a little bit, let your company have some float in the checking account. You may be in a great market right now that's just booming but someday it's going to have a little downturn.

A ton of companies go out of business because they didn't plan on ever having a downturn in their business. Businesses are cyclical: they're going to go up, they're going to go down.

If you have money in the bank you can withstand the little dips. You come back up and save a little more. You can take a little money out when times are good but don't take a lot of money out when times are bad. This way you'll be able to stand the cyclical ups and downs of business. The unfortunate part is that it's a zero sum game. If you get in a dip, no matter how good things look on the other side of the dip, if you run out of money, you're out.

In a casino, there's something called a house edge. Let's use Black Jack for our example and 6.4% as the house edge. If you played 1,000 hands of Black Jack and wagered $100 a hand, that's $100,000. The casino would make $6,400 just in a basic, statistical edge in gambling. Casinos would starve to death and couldn't operate if they only operated on that mathematical number.

However, they don't, because there's the drop factor. You run out of money before they do. People gamble their budget on the table whether things are good or bad. A good gambler will tell you that money management is the key to success over time: never betting more than 10% or 15% of their total bankroll at any one given setting at a gambling table. They don't make stupid decisions.

How many times have you been in a casino and said: "Man, I had a great run. Things were up. Then I had a little bad run and things were down. Then I ran out of money." Right there, you're out. If a guy walks up to a table with $1,000 bucks, has a bad run, and loses $1,000 in 20 minutes, think about that. It would take the casino hundreds and hundreds and hundreds and hundreds of hands at that 6.4% to make up that difference.

That's where businesses go out of business. You're running along and things are great. You're partying up, winning at the tables, drinking drinks, tipping the waitress and having fun – that's business.

However, when things start to dip, if you would have saved your drink and tip money and not have gone to that big fancy dinner that night, you might have been able to withstand the downturn at the table. Unfortunately, though, you ran out. Essentially you weren't reinvesting back into your business.

There's a great book that I recommend to anybody. It's called The Richest Man in Babylon. It's a fabulous little book, only about 20 or 30 pages long. Basically, it's a fable. It really explains this better than any story that I've ever seen. You can probably buy it on Amazon for five bucks. I used to give them away to people.

Other Sources Of Funding

If you're not going to go the VC route, you might want to try for a grant or loan. However, I have great news for you on both of those. You probably don't have to worry about either one as neither one will probably do you a lot of good.

Grant Proposals

There are a lot of scams out there about grants for businesses: "Get this grant, start your own business!" In reality, they are extremely rare and difficult to get. Grants are typically for non-profit or not-for-profit organizations. They call them 501(c)(3) corporations. They can get grant money. Also, religious organizations.

However, they typically don't give grants to "for profit" businesses. So, unless you're in the non-profit sector, you can kind of write that one off.

If you are in the non-profit sector, the best money that you'll ever spend is hiring a reputable grant writer – somebody that you've gotten as a recommendation from a local organization who have written a lot of grants before.

Loan Applications

What you need to tell them about your business in your loan application is how much your house is worth. That's really all they care about!

They don't want to hear about all of your dreams, aspirations, business plan, or how much money you're going to make. Most banks couldn't give you money for a business now even if they wanted.

Most banks, or formal lending institutions, really don't make business loans. They make "line of credit loans" after a business is established. For banks, business start-up loans are a thing of the past.

The only exception to that is probably Small Business Loans – SBA Loans, which is a program that the Federal government has. They guarantee business loans for small business owners through banks. So, you get the loan from the bank but the Federal government is guaranteeing the loan. That's a whole long, long talk about what to do to get an SBA loan. It's a mile long and a lot of paperwork to determine if they're going to give you that loan or not.

A lot has to do with your credit worthiness and what do you have that they can take if you don't pay the loan? They don't really care a whole lot about how terrific your idea is. They're really just collateral-based lenders.

If the business is doing well down the line and you have established credit, and you say: "I need 'X' amount of dollars to open up a new line or invest more money in sales," then you could get a line of credit. However, they're still going to absolutely insist that you have assets to back your credit rating. You may be able to use your credit line to buy assets – that's the way that you would get assets.

The old joke is that, "Banks only loan money to people who don't need it." It's kind of true. For the most part, you have to have a lot of assets to back it up.

Budget Flexibility

You need a budget but budgets have to be flexible based on sales. Again, let's go back to 64% of the businesses that fail.

People who set a budget decide how much money that they're going to spend, how many people they're going to employ, and how much they're going to spend on this or that.

Then in the downturn of the business they don't adjust their budget; they just run constant. The business is declining, sales are declining and income is declining but expenses stay solid. Eventually that breaks. You need to make sure that most of your budget is set to where it can be flexible to the performance of your company.

That's the reason that I like paying some of my employees with wages based on revenue. I like to make joint venture deals versus employee deals so that when sales are down, so are expenses. When sales are up, expenses are up. When sales are up and expenses are up, you don't care. When sales are down and expenses are down, you don't care. When sales are down and expenses are up, or flat, that's when you run into big problems.

That's the reason that a lot of bigger companies now are using a lot of part-time employees and temporary employees that they can lay off quickly without any repercussion. This is another good reason to use an employee leasing service.

Office Space 5

Buying Or Leasing?

When considering whether to buy or lease office space, ninety-nine percent of the time leasing is a better option. The only exception would be if you just have a lot of cash that you want to put somewhere or if you wanted to buy the business for speculation.

Buying a building is not the best option for businesses. You might wonder why giant corporations lease buildings instead of just buying them. It's because of expandability.

If you buy a building, you're stuck in the constraints of that building. You can't really expand or contract based on business needs, you can't change directions as fast.

If you have a two or three year lease and business trends down, you can drop a couple of your bays and lease a smaller space. If it gets bigger, you can lease five, six, or seven more bays and expand. If you have to build, you may be two years to build on another wing to your building and the ROI not be there - unless you're in the real estate business.

What a lot of business owners will do, if they have the cash, is build a building and lease it back to their own company. Again, you'd have to consult your attorney or accountant about it but I think there are some tax advantages to it. If you feel like you're going to be in business a long time, and it's performing well, it may be a fixed savings account for you almost. If you let your business pay off the building, then eventually – when you retire or sell or whatever – you'll own the building.

I've known some older people that have retired from selling buildings that they bought 30 or 40 years ago. They bought them to run a business out of, and then later retired. Their retirement is selling off a $3,000,000 or $4,000,000 building that's been paid off a long time ago.

However, I'd say 99% of the time, leasing is usually a better option.

Location

Location can be imperative for the success of business.

The old joke is: The three biggest rules of the retail business are: 1) location; 2) location; and 3) location. It's probably the most important thing.

A lot of people pick location as being how many cars drive by. They can be really wrong. You don't want to put a new French restaurant in the middle of the lowest income street in town just because it has 10,000 cars a day driving in front of it. You don't want to put a Chuck E. Cheese in a retirement community that has 100,000 cars driving in front of it. It doesn't matter.

What really matters is if you getting the foot traffic or drive-by traffic that you need from the right people – the people who are your potential target market.

Your Target Demographic 6

Creating a Profile

Profiling your target market is a really good thing to do. When I'm consulting business, I try to create a sheet on who my buyer is. We usually come up with a picture that we find on the Internet of who we think our average buyer is. We give her a name and guess what kind of work she does. We create a profile sheet.

Then when we hang that up on the wall we say:

> "Okay, let's look at a location. Would Mary Lou be in that part of town?"
>
> "No, not really. She wouldn't go out there."

"Would Mary Lou be in this kind of town?"

"Yes, there's a dress barn out there. She does crafts and there's a craft store. It's right next to the grocery store where she has to go two times a week. Yes, this is a great place."

You can kind of target it to the profile of whoever you think that your customer is.

Judge Your Competitors

If you're in retail, look at who they are, the cars that they drive, counties on their license plates – if they're rural and coming in from out of town. Do they drive a lot of pick-up trucks? Do they drive fancy sports cars? Are they younger? Are they in suits? Are they upwardly mobile professionals? You're going to be able to tell a lot from your competitors.

Purchase Demographic Data

There is demographic data that you can buy. If you're looking at residential networks there's a really neat website that I love. It's called www.ZipSkinny.com. You can enter any zip code in the country and it will give you all the latest pertinent demographic data on that zip code: the average median income; average number of men and women; etc.

I have a client that runs ice cream trucks. They do these demographic studies using www.ZipSkinny.com to see how many kids are in a neighborhood. If the total population of the neighborhood is more than 10% under nine years old, he runs his trucks in those neighborhoods. If they're not, he doesn't. He's running a terrific business by doing that. He's saving himself a lot of time and money, as he's able to target his market.

Advertise To Your Market

People say that advertising doesn't work. The truth is, in most people's cases, they're right. This is because 90 or 95% of the advertising dollar they spend is wasted on prospects that wouldn't be a customer of theirs no matter what.

If you're advertising on radio, television, newspapers, in a metro-market, or in a national market, it's almost even worse. For example, imagine you're advertising a brand new knee patch for arthritis. Well, maybe 95% of the people don't have arthritis. However, if you were advertising in a geriatric community to people that you got off the mailing list from an orthopedic specialist, what are your chances or odds of selling those people?

People will say it costs too much to get those leads. That doesn't matter, because 100% of your advertising message is going to the right person.

For the most part it needn't cost too much. Location if you're in retail is one thing. However, if you're in the lawn care business, for example, it doesn't matter where you have your trucks parked: that's not your location. The location is where you're going out marketing your services.

Direct Mail Advertising

Direct mail is my favorite form of advertising, and would be good for most start-up businesses because you can really target. If you do it right, it has almost zero waste.

Let's take the lawn care business as an example.

In the lawn care business you try to target neighborhoods where you have a gross median income of over $100,000. People who make a whole lot of money think their time is worth more than it is mowing grass so the potential for you to get these people to allow you to mow their grass is far higher than it is in a lower income area where a man thinks: “Well, I only make eight dollars an hour anyway; I’m not going to pay a kid ten dollars an hour to come and mow my grass. I’ll just mow it myself.” If the guy makes $80 an hour and he can get a kid to mow it for ten bucks an hour then in his mind, he’s saving $70. He can do something else and make more money.

So, say you want to only mow grass in the 70210 area code and you don’t want to be driving your truck all over town. These homes are well cared for, you’ve done the demographic and people there usually make a lot of money. Direct mail would allow you to target that demographic by economics.

Let's say that you were opening a model train store in your town. You could go buy the mailing list from Model Train magazine and only mail Model Train magazine subscribers that live in your town to tell them that you have a brand new train store opening or you could just sit there in your store at the back of the K-Mart on the wrong side of the street and wait until some of those people happen to drive by and see your sign. Which one do you think would be the better plan?

One last example: this is one of the neatest examples of direct mail that I've ever heard in my life. It's brilliant.

I know a man named Bill Myers, a smart-guy marketing guru. He's just a genius. He is a master at crossing markets.

Not too long ago they were selling a big gold coin promotion where they sold gold coins on television. You probably saw the commercials.

Bill found a source to buy hidden wall safes from. These wall safes were dirt-cheap. He bought them for ten bucks each when they cost $30 or $40 wholesale. He bought 2,000 or 3,000 wall safes.

Then he bought the customer list from the people on TV that sold the gold coins to people. He sent out a direct mail piece. The headline was something like:

> "Where Are You Hiding Your Gold Coins?"

As soon as they open the envelope, that's what it says:

> "Where Are You Hiding Your Gold Coins?"

Hey, wait a minute...

The next paragraph was:

> "Yes, I know that you have gold coins in your house. I know that you're probably hiding them somewhere that's not safe. Do you know how I found this out? I bought your name from a mailing list for seven cents. So could any criminal in your city. However, I have good news. For only $199, I can sell you this super amazing wall safe. You can hide it behind a picture or put it somewhere where no one would ever find it. You can keep your coins in there."

Isn't that a cool idea? That's a really great example of how you can use direct mail advertising to your advantage. If you do your research on the frontend, you can really increase your chances of succeeding.

I've seen it used in the gourmet pizza business, the dry cleaning business, lawn services, carpet cleaning services: there are a billion examples where direct mail can be effective. Oversized postcards are really good, too.

Goals 7

We were talking earlier about the VCs setting milestones and goals, but even if you don't get involved with VCs, you definitely still need goals.

Let's use Federal Express as an example. I'm very familiar with the Federal Express Corporation because I lived in Memphis, Tennessee, a long time. Every employee at Federal Express has to have a one-year, three-year, and five-year plan: every single employee. This plan includes where they're going to be in the company, what they're going to be doing for the company, what their division is going to be doing, what's it's going to be making, and how they're going to be contributing. They have to have a plan. That's been one of the biggest success secrets to Federal Express over the last 20 or so years. It's a great American success story.

Personal Goals and Reverse Engineering

Planning is extremely important as far as goal setting. However, I think that personal goal setting is even more important than even business goal setting. With a personal financial goal, it's easy to reverse engineer a problem.

If you say: "I'm going to make my company gross $10,000,000 a year," then keep that number in your face all the time – stick it everywhere you possibly can.

I'm the only guy that I know that takes baths; I don't take showers, I take baths. In the morning when I'm sitting back in the bathtub chilling, I have a framed piece of paper directly in front of me in my bathtub. I stare at it for 20 minutes a day.

It has a few goals on it. I make sure that they're in a place where I can see them.

I have them stuck on my mirror so that when I shave in the morning I can read them. Sometimes I put them on my computer as screensavers. I'll put them places that I can see them to remind me of a goal. It's amazing. If you'll say to yourself, "I have this business and this is what it can do."
Most people don't know what they want from their business. That's one of their biggest problems. They're just gliding through not knowing exactly what it is that they're looking for.

But then how do you know when you won? How do you know when you succeed if you don't set forth a goal?

What I would say is, set a goal that you think is reasonable, then double it, then double it one more time. Then post that goal. Say: "This is what I'm going to do." At that point, you don't even have to a plan as to how you're going to do it.

You should be uncomfortable with it. However, what you'll end up doing (usually in just a few days – it'll drive you nuts to stare at that, even for a few days) is starting to reverse engineer back how you can make that goal happen.

They teach kids to read. It's a tremendous thing that kids learn to read in the first grade. When you realize the complexity of what it takes for a child to take letters and turn them into words that are audible, and they do that in a year. It's incredible that they learn it.

However, they do it all in little bitty, tiny steps and they sort of reverse it. They show a kid a word, and then they show them how to decode it and how to recognize it by sight. They break down the problem; they reverse the problem.

They don't start with a blank sheet of paper and say: "Okay, now draw a word." They start with a word and reverse engineer it. They do a little bit at a time.

You're going to reverse engineer that problem out and work toward that goal. The good thing about setting high goals for yourself is that a lot of times, you'll hit them. That makes you feel good and more confident. But if you miss the goal that you set, if it was a high goal, sometimes where you missed it isn't all that bad.

Most people will achieve something slightly less than the goal that they set for themselves. Slightly less, but, not greatly less.

If you're willing to say: "You know, I could really get by on a thousand bucks a week" then you might end up making $700 or $800 a week.

If you say: “I’d really like to make $10,000 a month,” you might make $7,000 or $8,000. If you say: “I’d be kicking it out of the ball park. My goal in life is to make $50,000 a month.” Then what if you miss it by half? It still isn’t all that bad, you know?

Set high goals for yourself and reverse engineer back out.

Mental Banding

The biggest – absolutely the biggest – drawback to most people’s income, what keeps them from having the income they want, is right between their ears. They just don’t believe that they can do it.

They call it mental banding. There’s a guy named John Assaraf who has a book called ‘The Street Kid’s Guide to Having Everything’. He’s a really nice guy and a friend of mine. He shows mental banding: that most millionaires that go broke. Believe me, millionaires go broke. You can guess how I know this.

So millionaires go broke. It happens all the time. But most millionaires that go broke will be back to their previous income within 18 months. They usually will excel it considerably. They've already done it once and they know that they're capable of doing it. That's the big deal: they know that they're capable of doing it.

On the other side of the coin, most people who win multi-million dollar lotteries and take the lump sum payment and not the annual payouts end up broke and down back to their original income or below their original income within 18 months. It's a mental banding issue.

People that win the lotto will end up broke within 18 months because they snapped too quickly out of their comfort zone. They will do things that are absolutely self-destructive to get back to that comfort zone.

John's book teaches you how to stretch those bands. If you stretch a rubber band quite a lot, you exercise that band a lot, it becomes looser and looser and more malleable.

He grew up on the streets. He got into a lot of legal trouble when he was younger: petty crime stuff. He was basically just a thug. Now he's living in a 7,000 square foot house, hanging off the side of a cliff in San Diego. It overlooks his yacht.
He's doing real well and has learned. Everything that he's done is through superior mental conditioning.

You would be pretty much crazy to not be setting goals. It's like getting in a rowboat without a compass. You don't know where you're going to go; you're just floating out in the ocean. That will throw you into that 64% real quick.

Written Goals

Harvard University did a 20-year study. It was of people who had graduated from Harvard 20 years ago. However, before they graduated, they surveyed each one of them about their plan for life: "What's your plan for life? What are you going to do? What are your goals?"

Only six percent of the class had written goals on what they were going to do with their life, what they were going to achieve. They actually had finite measurements of it, by a certain time. The rest didn't.

They tracked these people over the years and 20 years later a percentage of them were dead, a small percentage of the Harvard graduates were living in poverty, and most were living fairly average lives. The six percent of people who had written goals had a higher gross net worth than the other 320 people in the class combined.

This really shows how important written planning is. If you don't write it it's as if it doesn't exist. When I set expectations for people in goals in business, I like to ask them to write their plan out and sign it just like a contract. You can sign a contract with yourself. Stick that up on your wall to remind you. You need to look in the mirror while you're doing it.

Facing Yourself In The Mirror

Another guy that I love to read is Robert Cialdini. He has a book called Influence: The Psychology of Persuasion. He does all of these social experiments.

One of them was with kids and Halloween. They let kids come in the house and get the candy out of the bowl. They said: "Please only take one piece." There was no one around so when the kids went to the bowl of candy, they'd grab a fist full of candy and take off out the door. About 60% of the kids took more than one piece of candy.

Then they put a great big mirror up on either side of the candy bowl so that they couldn't take candy from the bowl any way except facing a mirror. Then only about 12% of the kids took more than one piece of candy.

One time I met a management guy. He was a troubleshooter – a guy who fixed companies. He went into some big companies to fix them, such as Dow Chemical. When Dow Chemical had a plant that was just screwed up, they called him. They brought him in by helicopter to fix this plant. Sometimes the company was losing up to $500,000 a day. His fees were not cheap.

The first thing that he would do was call them in advance: "I'm going to be there tomorrow morning at seven o'clock. I want you to call a glass company. I want behind my desk to be completely mirrored."

When he was talking to an employee sitting across his desk, he always positioned himself so that he was to one side or the other of them. This was so that when they answered him they had to be looking into the mirror. He said: "I always got the truth."

Perhaps you're auditory and you read aloud your goals. When you do, read them out staring directly into a mirror and read eye-to-eye. It makes it a little difficult, but if you do that on a regular basis, you'll begin to achieve those goals.

It's going to penetrate into you. And it is going to be uncomfortable for a while.

Customer Service 8

You Are Your Business

The most important thing to your business is that you become a trusted friend to your clients. Your business is you, it really is.

It seems like people are either happy or mad with gigantic companies. How many times have you heard somebody say: "Boy, I'd sure like to kick Bill Gates in the ass right now" because they're mad at their Windows or Microsoft product? Or: "Steve Jobs is a genius"? They recognize these personalities that have to do with businesses.

Faceless corporations have a harder time growing. As an individual or small business owner, one of your biggest advantages is being able to be personal. It's an advantage for you, especially in a world that's becoming more and more and more impersonal. People want interpersonal communications.

Have you ever heard of Crazy Eddie? I'll never forget those Crazy Eddie commercials. If you go to YouTube and look up "Crazy Eddie" you can see some of them. He used to shoot TVs with shotguns and do all kinds of crazy nutty stuff:

> "I'm Crazy Eddie and I'm crashing wild prices!"

People in New York loved him because he was a New Yorker and kind of nuts. He became a giant celebrity on TV from selling electronics. He made millions and millions and millions of dollars.

There are still guys out there that do those kinds of things, especially in the car business. People want to know you. People like to do business with people that they like.

If you have a handshake policy with your customers, you want to make sure that you shake the hand of everyone in your store:

> "Hey. My name's Nathan. I just want to tell you that I appreciate you coming into my store. I thank you so much. This is how I support my family. If I can do anything for you, I'll do it because you're doing a lot for me by just being here. Thank you."

Thank your customers; they're the reason that you exist.

Remove The Poison

Some people get bitter about their customers. If that behavior starts in your company, pluck it out immediately. Don't tolerate it for five seconds;

pluck it out. Do it publicly in front of a lot of people: "This is not going to happen here."

I have another parable of great advice. It's one of the best pieces of advice that I received about running a company. A great manager told me one time: "There's nothing in the world that will ruin a great employee faster than watching you tolerate a poor one."

That sends a really strong message. It kills their motivation to be any better. You can actually destroy a great employee because if they're getting the same benefits, money, et cetera, that a crappy employee is getting, they may ask: "Why am I wasting my time trying to do a good job?"
You set the tone. In a sense, it's the culture that you create. You need to fire a person that's treating your customers poorly. You'll then find that, overall, your people will be happier, too. They'll

be glad to see that person go. They know; everybody knows. You have to remove the poison.

Andrew Carnegie fired a guy one time. This man had made Mr. Carnegie a hundred million dollars a year – it was a crazy amount of money back then. It's a lot now; but, back then it was a ton, ton, ton of money. He fired him because he was unpalatable to the other people around him. He was a real jerk and he cold fired him.

He said that within the year he made back way more money but for a while it was tough. He said: "If you let that poison stay, it'll kill everything." It's a weed, it's a parasite, and it has to go.

For the most part, as long as you lead by example and tightly monitor what's going on, you can do well.

I'll tell you a great example that I heard just recently. It's from the President of Zappos, an online shoe store. They've done remarkable things. They have 1,600 sales representatives on the phone selling shoes to ladies online that they haven't seen. You have to do a great job to do that.

They have a policy that I found extremely interesting: after you've trained with them for three weeks, they come into the room, and say:

> "Now, you've been with us for three weeks. You only have another week or two of training left. At this point, we'd like to make you an offer. We're willing to write a $1,000 check to anyone that wants to quit. If you'll quit right now, we'll give you $1,000. It's in the hallway. Just walk outside and ask for your check."

If the person isn't committed enough to the company by then, then they don't want them. They figure that that person is going to cost them a lot more than $1,000. They haven't bought into the Zappos lifestyle. They're not wearing the Zappos shoes, they're not singing the company song to their kids when they go to bed at night, they haven't bought into the culture. If they haven't bought into the culture, they don't want them there. Period.

Running Your Business 9

Mission Statements

You want to establish the kind of culture where people are motivated and excited to be there.

People would always say to me: “What’s your mission statement?” and until very, very recently I always thought that was a bunch of crap:

> “I don’t have a mission statement. What do you mean a mission statement? My mission statement is to make money.”

I thought it was a terrible idea. However, people will follow you to the moon for a cause. You buying another Ferrari is not a cause. They don’t mind you having the Ferrari, but people want to feel like they're doing something good. They want to be a part of something bigger than themselves. If you're going to be in business you need to be doing something that brings great benefit to your customers. If you don't, you're just not going to be around long. The truth of it is, you're wasting your time. Go and get a job. You're really just not going to be around long.

If that's the kind of thing that you have going on, you will burn through employees like wildfire. They understand what they're doing. If you're just: "rack them, sack them, and pack them" then in the back of your employee's minds they know that they're not going to have a job for very long, because you're not going to have a business very long. They never feel grounded and secure.

Zappos also does one more thing. They give each customer service representative a budget so that they can do nice things for customers. For instance, if a customer just had a rotten experience – something just really bad happened – they can send a customer flowers, cookies, a little gift, etc. They may send something that costs five dollars; they may send something that cost $50.

One of the things that made Zappos famous was that one of their sales reps sent flowers. There was a lady who had called and wanted to return some shoes. It was past the due date but it was because she had bought them for her mother and she had passed away from cancer. She said: “I’m really sorry that I didn’t return these at the right time. I really hope that I can still get a refund.”

The next day, her doorbell rang. It was the UPS man there to pick up the package of shoes. He also dropped off a giant package of shoes and gifts for her. Later that day it was followed by flowers and condolences for the loss of her mother from the staff of Zappos.

It became famous and imagine the pride of the employees – "I work for that kind of company. That's the kind of company that I work for." With that kind of company and culture, you almost don't have to give them extra cash because they're part of something that they're truly proud to be a part of.

I can tell you from past experience that money instead of good customer service just does not work. It just doesn't work. People are okay working with an hourly job but they want to be appreciated in the job that they do, have something interesting, and be working towards something that helps people make their lives better. And what makes a woman's life better other than new shoes?!

Successful Leadership

Being a good leader is about being willing to get down and do the job that you would expect anybody to do. It's not that you should be spending your time doing that but having a willingness to do that is good.

Not too long ago I was at dinner and sat next to a guy that had worked for Federal Express Corporation. He had his Employee ID card from Federal Express with his employee number on it. Currently, the employees for Federal Express are up around 350,000. He was number seven.
He had a picture that he carried in his wallet – imagine this. It was a picture of a bunch of guys and him. They were standing in front of an airplane and they were all holding something in their hands.

He said: “Do you know what that picture is?”

I said: “No. What?”

He said:

> “That was a Falcon Regional Jet. It was one of the first planes that we had in Federal Express. We’re standing in front of the plane and all of us are holding our credit cards because we used our own personal credit cards to fill it up with jet fuel. There wasn’t any money in the Federal Express account to buy fuel for the plane and we had to get it across the country.”

He said that if he had anything in his life that he could do over again, he would go back and do that start-up with Fred Smith and that group of guys again. It was the most exciting time of his life.

He knew that they were doing something that was going to change the world. That's what people want. Not the extra cash. That extra little bit of cash is not going to make a difference to you when you're all sitting in your rocking chairs and telling stories. The person that wants the extra cash is like the person who will take the $1,000 check and leave.

Balancing Work And Life

If you are thinking about setting up a business you need to think at the outset how you're going to go about balancing a successful business and raising your family at the same time. If you're married, you need to talk to your spouse before you ever start because this is a commitment. When you start a business, it's a commitment and can be all encompassing.

If you are a lady who is starting a business, I think it's harder on you sometimes. I think that husbands have higher expectations of their wives than wives have of their husbands. Wives know that we're not worth a hoot for anything.

Husbands have expectations like: "What do you mean dinner isn't here? What do you mean I have to take the kids to school this morning?"

You have to really sit down and have a talk and have the support of your mate. By "talk," I mean a heart-to-heart one because when you're starting a business from scratch this isn't something that's going to be over with in two weeks. It's going to take awhile.

You're going to really have to dig in and know that sometimes you won't be there: you're going to miss dinner, your mind is going to be preoccupied in what you're doing. There are no weekends off any more. No more: “I go to work at nine o’clock and get off at five o’clock.”

Instead, you’re going to do whatever has to be done until it’s done or until you can’t any more. A lot of the time you’ll work from the time you can in the morning until you can’t at night.
However, a lot of people get into a business and abuse that. Like: “I can’t take out the garbage, I have to go to work” or “I don’t want to go to your mother’s this weekend because I have to work.” They can abuse that a lot.

I would say that if you’re in a relationship with somebody who is tolerating you being in the business, don’t abuse them. It’s a tough place to be, it’s hard, especially if they don’t completely understand what you’re doing.

I’d say that one of the biggest things to do is to keep them really involved. If you can, go ahead and play this audio for your spouse. Let them know how important it is that they be interested in what you're doing. If they aren't interested and you're going solo, it is a tough place to be. I've seen both men and women make it but it's really hard on the relationship. The key is to find balance .Being able to stay positive and keep a strong mindset when you're building a business are really key ingredients too.

Franchises 10

Believe it or not, there are a lot of advantages to franchises. I used to giggle and say: "That guy's too dumb to get in business. He has a franchise."

However, on the whole, franchises fail at a much, much, much lower rate than do normal start-up businesses. The reason that they fail is because they do the things that we've covered here.

Franchise Benefits

They're systemized. A good franchise knows who its customer is. It has a product or service that is unique to its marketplace and a management plan where everyone knows what they're supposed to do. They deliver a product well. They typically have ways of generating additional income. They also have loyalty programs and get people to come back into their businesses.

Today people think: “Well, I’ll just open a store like my grandpa did. He had a store. He just put stuff out on a shelf and people came in and bought it.”

He did, but he was probably the only store in a 20-mile radius. Not so much the shiny apple as the rotten apple in the middle of the dessert to a starving crowd. If you had a starving herd of people and if the apple had a little bad spot on it, you’d just cut it out with a knife and eat the apple anyway. In some parts of America and especially in other parts of the world, a rotten apple would do just fine. It’s going to do okay because people have to have something.

Local Competition

We live in Austin, Texas. Austin has more clever business entrepreneurs than in any city I've ever seen and I've traveled the world extensively. They have more brilliant concepts and great advertising marketing methods. It's a fabulous city. If you get a chance to come to Austin, drive around and look at the businesses, the ads from Austin, and at the newspapers and radio stations and see how cool it is.

The thing is it's a really competitive marketplace of really smart and creative people, so you have to be cool. You can't just be the shiny apple in Austin. You have to be the shiny apple half-dipped in part caramel and half-dipped in chocolate with cashews sprinkled on the top on a glittery stick. With a cool t-shirt and a name. You have to be

“Apple-icious” or something. You can’t just be the apple guy; you have to be excellent.

You can put on a little play in Austin and people will come. It’ll be okay. They won’t throw tomatoes on you, even if you kind of suck. In Lincoln, Nebraska, you can suck real bad and they’re not going to throw tomatoes on you. However, if you go to Broadway in New York, you better have it together. You need to have rehearsed and have skill and talent.

If you’re going to play music in downtown Austin, you better be pretty good. If you’re going to go to Nashville and try to cut a record as a country artist, you better be pretty good. If you’re going to go to California and be a movie actress, you better be beautiful. Which place is better to be beautiful in? California or Kansas? It all depends. You can be a big fish in a little pond.

The franchise business is basically like taking the prettiest girl in California to Kansas. You could take business concepts in Austin to Mississippi and they're going to look great because they may not be as progressive there. The same thing probably applies to a conservative Midwestern town.

However, sometimes you can be too wacky and it doesn't work. There is some real wacky stuff in Austin which wouldn't work in too conservative an environment.

The number one rule of marketing is standing out, being different. However, these franchises have learned how to work in different demographic areas.

I think that Starbucks do some franchising, but I don't know for sure. However, if they did franchise, it would be a great one because they pick their audience well demographically. They choose colors of those places. They say: “Is this color friendlier than another color?” They may paint four stores in four different colors in four similar demographic spots to see which one does more sales and traffic. That’s called split testing.

Learn From Their Mistakes

So, a franchise is somebody who has taken a local business, made a model, got it to where it was optimum, and then took it out and opened two or three more to prove that the model would work somewhere else. Now they want to expand their business by taking on franchise partners.

As a franchisee, you’re fundamentally a partner with a franchising company. It’s just a method for them to expand their business. The advantages for you are that they’ve made all the mistakes.

Let me tell you what gets the "Dumb-Dumb of the Year" award – it's the guys (and I know a ton of them) who have bought a franchise, got in there and then said: "Oh, I'm not going to do that that way. That's just dumb." People do that all the time.

> "I've been in the restaurant business for 20 years and Subway says that I have to sell this garlic cheese bread? I'm not going to sell that stuff. I don't think anyone is going to buy it. I'm not going to make it."

Subway may have tested that and that's the best selling bread of all. The guy just doesn't know it because he's never tried it.

Guesswork sucks. The market will tell you what it wants. If you open a restaurant, put out five different kinds of bread, and ask your customers what kind of bread they would like. Eventually there will be one or two kinds of bread that will be

80% of your market. Then go ahead and get rid of the other three. However, I would almost bet that you won't know in advance what those two will be. It's almost never the ones that you guess. I've been doing this a long time and it's almost never the ones that I guess.

The advertising and direct mail guys say that the best guys in the industry are right about 55% of the time. The odds of Johnny Greenhorn hitting it on the first swing at bat are pretty low.

If you can afford it, buy a franchise in the industry that you're in but research it well first. My best advice to you would be to talk to some of the franchise owners first.

I certainly don't bust on franchises any more. I've seen a lot of people be extremely successful with them. I would probably recommend them in most industries.

Drawbacks

There are a few drawbacks though. The biggest one is money. Most franchises have a flat fee but I wouldn't worry about that too much. They're going to earn that fee because they'll come in to teach you their business model: you're basically buying their system.

However, the ongoing fees can be expensive. The restrictions that they have for buying certain supplies from them can be restrictive. Even though they might say 5%, 7%, 10%, whatever the franchise fee is, what really happens in most cases is an even 50-50 split of the profit at the end of the year. Again, this happens most of the time with a franchise company.

It is a little painful but they've got a proven business model and you don't. It's like being the entrepreneurial part of the business. You just have to deal with it.

Honestly, for entrepreneurs I don't know that franchises are that great an idea. A person with a real strong entrepreneurial mindset tends to want to change things. They tend to want to do things their way.

If you've been a successful manager before, a franchise is a great idea. This is because you don't have to give up the day-to-day running of the business, profit, etc to an entrepreneurial type. You don't really need it. The franchise, if they're a successful one, is going to tell you everything that you need to do. You just need to follow and manage their system. If you can do that effectively, you can be successful as a franchisee.

The Entrepreneurial Mindset 11

Not just anyone can be an entrepreneur, although I'd sell a lot more stuff if I told everyone they could!

If you're starting a business from scratch, it's a concept and I believe that you have to be entrepreneurial to make it work. Not everybody is entrepreneurial. I think that a lot of people are just born with that gene, that entrepreneur bone.

However, if you're a management person, not very creative, and don't have a lot of vision, then go out and hire someone that is, then you can be involved. Then you can do it.

If the question is: "Can anybody set up a successful business by themselves?" then my answer is no. However, if it's: "Can anybody do it with the help of someone else?" then it is yes. There are a lot of people who are entrepreneurs who can manage well enough to get by. There are also managers who have a little entrepreneurial spirit and they can get by. Those two examples can be solo acts.

However, if you're just totally entrepreneurial, then you have a real high chance of failure, even if your idea is absolutely brilliant. If you can't get it executed properly, it means nada, so respect your management partner or management people.

If you're a great entrepreneur and you have financial means, hire a manager. They are everywhere that you look. You don't have to give them half of your money. If you're entrepreneurial, you can pay him a flat fee to run the business. You can run it well enough to get it started then hire a manager to run it for a flat fee. Then you can keep the bull's share of the money.

However, one of the biggest things that entrepreneurial people do (or managers or people in business do) is to expect an employee who is on a relatively flat fee basis to be as concerned, worried, and into their business as they are. That's an absolute recipe for failure because most people aren't going to be.

If you're on a particular mission, then yes. They can be as fired up about your mission as you are, if not more so. For example, you can get Presidential or Gubernatorial candidates who are running for offices that have campaign volunteers that are more passionate about their campaign than they are. They bought into the dream, hook, line, and sinker, and they're committed.

Honestly, people want to be committed to something: we need it. It's a primal need that we have. We need a mission in life. We need a purpose.

Good luck in all your endeavors.

Book Recommendations 12

There are a million great books out there on how to start a business.

The Triad Marketing System (www.TriadMarketingSystem.com)

A marketing product which really does go in depth in the three ways of marketing. It gives you a great marketing education.

Think and Grow Rich by Napoleon Hill.

This is one of the books that changed my life is It's an old book that was written in the 20s. Don't judge it by its age; its wisdom is ageless. I think they did a survey not too long ago. They asked 1,000 multi-millionaires for their favorite book, the one that was most influential in their life. Think and Grow Rich was on about 75% of their lists. It was normally toward the top, too.

The Millionaire Mindset: How to Tap Real Wealth From Within by T. Harv Eker

A really great book about how to mentally condition yourself to prepare for financial greatness and leadership.

Good To Great Good To Great by Jim Collins.

A fabulous book which talks about how companies go from being good companies to being great companies. It talks about the principles and the culture. We talked a little bit about culture today. It's going to really go in-depth about the culture of building a business that becomes a great, mission-driven one.

The E-Myth Revisited by Michael E. Gerber

This book is all about the entrepreneurial spirit versus management-minded people. It also talks about how to get the most out of your entrepreneurial abilities and how to understand and work with other people around you.

Index

Made in the USA
Lexington, KY
16 January 2012